BEFORE I MADE HISTORY

Take a Stand, Rosa Parks!

by Peter and Connie Roop

SCHOLASTIC INC.

New York   Toronto   London   Auckland   Sydney
Mexico City   New Delhi   Hong Kong   Buenos Aires

For Heidi, who stands up for her beliefs!

ISBN 0-439-67625-8

12 11 10 9 8 7 6 5 4 3   5 6 7 8 9 10/0

Printed in the U.S.A.   40
First printing, February 2005

Contents

Introduction

Rosa Parks is famous for refusing to give up her seat on a bus. Do you know that Rosa felt her best achievement was helping young people?

Rosa Parks was born in 1913. Do you know that her grandparents were slaves when they were born?

Rosa Parks loved to learn. Do you know that Rosa could read before she went to school?

Rosa Parks went to a one-room school-house. Do you know that Rosa's school had no glass windows?

Rosa Parks was a hard worker. Do you know that Rosa picked cotton when she was only six years old?

Rosa Parks was good at making things with her hands. Do you know that Rosa often earned a living sewing clothes?

Rosa Parks enjoyed school. Do you know that Rosa quit high school to take care of her beloved grandmother when she was sick?

Rosa Parks didn't go to college. Do you know that she received many special college degrees for her civil rights work?

Rosa Parks liked to save things and use them again. Do you know that her nieces and nephews called Rosa "The Recycling Queen"?

Rosa Parks is famous for her courage as an adult. Do you know that Rosa was also very brave as a young person?

The answers to these questions lie in who Rosa Parks was as a young person before she made history.

1

Rosa Parks Is Born

The skies were clear on Tuesday, February 4, 1913. This winter day was unusually warm for Tuskegee, Alabama. A baby girl was crying inside the McCauleys' wooden house. Rosa Louise McCauley had just been born. Rosa was very small for a newborn infant. Her mother, Leona, rocked Rosa to make her stop crying. Her father, James, smiled at his daughter, the McCauleys' first child.

Leona and James had no idea that one day tiny Rosa would change history.

Rosa was named after her grandmother Rose Percival. Grandmother Rose had been born a slave in 1860. Rose was only five years old when the Civil War ended in 1865.

All African-American slaves were finally freed the following December.

Rose's parents, Mary Jane and James Percival, continued to live on the farm where they had been slaves. They lived in the same small log cabin. They did the same jobs. But life was different. The Percivals were paid for their work. They could own land for the first time in their lives. And they were free. They could move if they wished to.

The Percivals saved every penny. They bought twelve acres of land so they could have their own farm. Rose Percival began working for the Hudson family when she was six years old. Rose's job was to help take care of the Hudsons' baby. Young Rose did such a good job that the Hudsons gave her family six acres of land. The Percivals now had eighteen acres. They grew cotton to sell, raised their own chickens and cows, and harvested their own fruits and vegetables.

When he was a slave, James Percival made furniture for his master, Mr. Wright. When he was free, James made things for his own family. Young Rose held a burning torch at night so her father could work after dark. Once, James made a small wooden table for his family to eat on. James didn't use expensive iron nails for his table. Instead he drilled holes, carved wooden pegs, and tapped them into the holes to hold the table together. James made his table so well that Rosa Mc-Cauley used it as she grew up. When Rosa McCauley became Rosa Parks, she still used her great-grandfather's wooden table. Today this table has a special spot in Rosa's home.

Rosa's grandfather Sylvester Edwards had been born a slave just like her grandmother. Sylvester was freed at the end of the Civil War. Life was difficult for Sylvester. His parents died when he was young. Mr. Battle, the man who ran the farm where Sylvester lived, was very mean to him. Sometimes he hit Sylvester. One day, he hit Sylvester so hard that he hurt Sylvester's leg. He couldn't walk without limping.

Mr. Battle gave Sylvester very little food. Fortunately, the kitchen workers felt sorry for Sylvester. They saved food scraps for him. They gave Sylvester food when Mr. Battle wasn't looking.

Mr. Battle wouldn't let Sylvester have any shoes. In the summer, the burning dirt hurt Sylvester's feet when he worked in the cotton fields. Mr. Battle's behavior caused Sylvester Edwards to develop a dislike for white people. When he was older, Sylvester often stood up to white people even if it meant possibly getting into trouble.

Later, when Rosa Parks was famous for standing up for herself, she wrote, "My grandfather was the one who instilled in my mother and her sisters, and in their children, that you don't put up with bad treatment from anybody." Young Rosa McCauley learned that lesson well. As she grew up, she became tired of such bad treatment. Rosa's actions one day would change the history of the United States. Rosa's brave stand also influenced people around the world.

2
Rosa Moves

Rosa McCauley was a small child. She was often sick. Rosa said, "I came along and I was a sickly child, small for my age." Rosa needed special care from her mother, especially when her tonsils were infected. Sometimes Rosa would be in bed for days. It was hard for her to swallow because her throat hurt so much.

Rosa's mother was a schoolteacher. She had to take time from her work to care for Rosa. She comforted Rosa. She read to Rosa. She sang songs like "Oh, Freedom, Let It Ring" to Rosa. Rosa's mother, Leona, had been raised to always work to improve herself. Leona loved to learn. She enjoyed school and became a teacher. Her parents, Rose and Sylvester Edwards, encouraged Leona to get a good education. They didn't want her to cook and clean for white families.

The Edwards believed teaching was an important job. Black teachers didn't make as much money as white teachers did, but teaching paid more than cooking and cleaning. And teaching fellow African Americans would help their race, too.

Leona worked hard, went to college, and got her teaching certificate. Leona took a job teaching in the African-American school in Pine Level, Alabama. Leona lived at home with her parents on their farm.

One day, pretty Leona met handsome James McCauley from Abbeville, Alabama. James was a skilled bricklayer and carpenter. James traveled around building homes. James and Leona were married on April 12, 1912. This was the same day that the *Titanic* set sail. The McCauleys were married in the Mount Zion African Methodist Episcopal Church in Pine Level. James and Leona were twenty-four years old.

Before long, the newlyweds moved to

Tuskegee, Alabama. Beautiful Tuskegee was an important town for African Americans. Tuskegee was the home of the famous Tuskegee Institute. Booker T. Washington had founded this school for African Americans. Mr. Washington was an energetic man who believed that African Americans should be well educated. He also wanted all Americans, black and white, to learn to get along together.

Rosa's mother was happy to live in Tuskegee. She knew Tuskegee was the best place in Alabama for African Americans to get a good education. Leona wanted an excellent education for Rosa. Mrs. McCauley wanted Rosa to go to the Tuskegee Institute when she was older. But Rosa's father wanted to build houses near his own family back in Abbeville, Alabama. So baby Rosa and her parents moved to Abbeville.

The three McCauleys lived with James's large family. Leona returned to teaching now that others could take care of young Rosa. There were many children for Rosa to play with. Rosa enjoyed all of the hustle and bustle of the big family. But Rosa's mother didn't. The house was too noisy and crowded for her. She didn't like the fact that four children shared one room with a dirt floor.

One day, Rosa's father decided to move again, but this time by himself. He would build houses farther north. Rosa's mother decided to leave Abbeville. Rosa and her mother went to Pine Level to live with Leona's parents on their farm. Leona was happy to be back with her parents. Two-year-old Rosa was happy to be with her loving grandparents.

Rosa's father came to Pine Level for a little while but left again to find work. He came home every so often until Rosa was five years old. Then Mr. McCauley left for good. Rosa didn't see her father again until after she was married and was Rosa Parks.

Rosa's mother began teaching again. There was already a black teacher in Pine Level, so Mrs. McCauley took a teaching job eight miles away in Spring Hill, Alabama. Spring Hill was too far away for Rosa's

mother to teach, prepare her lessons, and go back and forth every day. So on Sunday afternoons, Grandfather Sylvester drove Rosa's mother to Spring Hill in his wagon. She lived with another family all week. Then Grandfather Sylvester drove back on Friday afternoons to bring her home to Pine Level.

At first, Rosa was confused as to why her mother kept leaving. She asked her grandmother, "Is Mama Leona going to learn how to teach school?" Grandmother Rose answered, "No, she's been teaching school since before you were born, so she's just going to teach school." Rosa understood, but she missed her mother all week long.

3

Rosa Grows

Rosa liked living with her grandparents. They took her fishing when she was big enough to hold a pole. Rosa became an expert at putting wiggling worms on fishhooks. Rosa was shy and liked playing by herself. But she also enjoyed playing with other children. Rosa liked to turn over rocks in a stream with her friends to catch quick crayfish scurrying to safety. She had to be fast to catch the crayfish and careful not to get pinched by their tiny snapping claws. Rosa enjoyed eating the captured crayfish when they were boiled like little lobsters and served with fresh corn.

Rosa also enjoyed the foods they grew on their farm. Her grandmother fried thick slices of ham. She fried the catfish Rosa helped catch. Sometimes Grandfather Sylvester trapped a rabbit, which Grandmother Rose cooked. Rosa enjoyed turnip greens, peas, and onions she had planted and harvested. Rosa especially enjoyed her grandmother's sweet potato pie.

Rosa liked listening to the stories her grandparents told while they were working or before bed at night. Grandmother Rose told stories about being a little girl during the Civil War. Rosa's grandfather told about how he had been so mistreated when he was young. From an early age, Rosa knew she wanted to be treated fairly.

Rosa, however, was often sick. Her tonsils would get infected and hurt her throat. But Rosa was brave. One day, when her tonsils were swollen, Grandfather Sylvester took Rosa into town to see a doctor. The doctor didn't have an office. He saw his patients at a store. Rosa remembers wearing her red velvet coat and a bonnet when she went to see the doctor. The doctor put Rosa on the counter. He asked her to open her mouth. The doctor used a spoon to hold down Rosa's tongue while he looked at her aching tonsils. Rosa did everything the doctor asked her to. She was very well behaved and used her best manners. When Rosa got home, Grandfather Sylvester bragged about brave little Rosa. Rosa enjoyed her grandfather's praise. She said, "I felt happy because he thought I was such a good little girl."

Rosa's mother knew Rosa would feel better if her tonsils were taken out. But Mrs. McCauley couldn't afford the cost of Rosa going to a hospital in another town. So Rosa put up with infected tonsils and sore throats, especially during the chill, damp winters.

When Rosa was almost three years old, her brother, Sylvester, was born. Rosa loved her little brother. She played with him. She helped him. She watched him so he wouldn't hurt himself. Sylvester adored his big sister. When he could walk, Sylvester followed Rosa everywhere she went. When Rosa said something, Sylvester repeated her words.

Sylvester, however, sometimes got into trouble. Rosa often tried to stop her grandmother from punishing him. But sometimes Rosa was punished for not telling her grandparents about the trouble Sylvester had gotten into.

All of their lives, Rosa and Sylvester were close companions. With their mother away teaching and their father gone, they depended on each other for love and support.

One day, when Rosa was five or six years old, she had a very interesting experience. She remembered this all her life. That day, in 1919, a white soldier returning from World War I stopped by Rosa's house. Rosa impressed him so much that the soldier patted Rosa on her head. He told Rosa that she was "a cute little girl." In those days in Alabama, it was very unusual for a white man to compliment a black child. Rosa felt good about being treated just like a normal human being. Rosa knew she was as good as anyone else, no matter what her color was.

4
Rosa Goes to School

Rosa loved books. Before she could read, Rosa would look at the pictures in a book. She made up stories to go along with the pictures. Rosa knew how to read before she went to school. Her mother taught Rosa at home when she was only four years old!

When she was older, Rosa enjoyed the book *Up from Slavery* by Booker T. Washington. Mr. Washington's autobiography told about how he had been born a slave and grew up to become a famous teacher. And it was Mr. Washington who started the Tuskegee Institute that Rosa's mother wanted her to attend.

Rosa and her mother especially liked Booker T. Washington's words about saving money, being thrifty, being neat, and working hard. All her life, Rosa was good at saving and reusing things. Rosa's nieces and nephews lovingly called her "The Recycling Queen."

Rosa also admired George Washington Carver. Mr. Carver, an African American, was an expert on plants. He taught at the Tuskegee Institute. Today, Mr. Carver is famous for his work in finding hundreds of uses for peanuts. George Washington Carver believed that everything on Earth had a purpose. Rosa took his words to heart. As a little girl, Rosa collected pine needles. She saved cornhusks. Rosa used the needles and husks to make little baskets.

Rosa grew up in a family that went to church. The Bible was an important book in Rosa's home. Rosa memorized many Bible verses. When she was older, Rosa relied on these Bible verses to comfort her when times were tough. She said, "Its [the Bible's] teaching became a way of life and helped me with my day-to-day problems."

Because Rosa was so small and frequently sick, she didn't go to school until she was six years old. Rosa started at the African-American school by her church in Pine Level. Rosa's school had only one room. There were sixty students, six grades, but only one teacher. There were no desks. The students sat in rows arranged by age. The school had windows, but no glass in the windows. There were shutters to close when it got cold.

Rosa's school was heated with wood the black community brought to the school. They took care of their own school. African Americans paid taxes just like white people. But none of that money went to Rosa's school. The money went to the white children's school. Black children and white children were not allowed to go to the same schools together. The government said schools could be "separate but equal." The black and the white schools were indeed separate, but they definitely were not equal!

Miss Sally Hill was Rosa's first teacher.

Rosa thought Miss Hill was very nice. Rosa especially appreciated Miss Hill's help when Rosa was teased for being so small. Miss Hill would hug and comfort Rosa. Rosa really enjoyed reading more books in school. She liked fairy tales and Mother Goose rhymes. When Miss Hill gave Rosa a new book to read, Rosa sat down and read the whole book at once! Rosa also learned to count and to write her letters.

Miss Hill left Rosa's school the next year. In second grade, Rosa had Miss Beulah McMillan for a teacher. Miss Beulah had also taught Rosa's mother. Rosa continued to like school and did well. Even though Rosa was shy, she joined in games at recess. Rosa really liked playing "Ring Around the Roses" and "Little Sally Walker Sitting in a Saucer" with her friends. Rosa learned many things in school. She also learned many lessons out of school. Rosa never forgot some of these lessons.

5
Rosa Learns
Other Lessons

One lesson Rosa learned was the difference between her school and the school for white children. Each morning, Rosa and her brother, Sylvester, walked past the school for white children. It had a playground. It even had glass windows. Rosa saw that her one-room school wasn't as big as the school that white children went to. Rosa's school wasn't new like the other school. But Rosa was lucky. She lived close to her school, so she didn't have to walk very far. Other African-American children had to walk much farther. Rosa learned that only white students could ride a bus to school each day.

Rosa learned that she would only go to

school five months a year. Black children stayed home in the spring to plant crops and in the early fall to help with the harvest.

Rosa learned another lesson on the way to school. When she and Sylvester walked to school, the bus carrying the white children would pass them. Sometimes the white children yelled mean names at Rosa and her brother, or threw trash at them. Rosa and Sylvester walked in nearby fields when they heard the school bus coming. Black people had no one to stand up for them to make things better. Rosa said, "It was just a matter of survival — like getting off the road — so we could exist from day to day."

All of these unfair things made Rosa feel she wasn't really free to be herself. She said, "By the time I was six, I was old enough to realize we were not exactly free."

When Rosa was six years old, many African-American soldiers came home from World War I. While they were away from Alabama, these brave men had experienced greater freedom and less discrimination.

They asked for better treatment at home. They asked for equal rights. Many white people didn't want blacks and whites to be equal. They believed in laws that kept blacks and whites separate. Nicknamed "Jim Crow" laws, these laws were named after a black character in a play, named Jim Crow. It was a Jim Crow law that said that Rosa couldn't go to school with white children because she was black.

Jim Crow laws said that black people had to sit in the balcony in a movie theater, not on the main floor with white people. Jim Crow laws said blacks couldn't play in *whites only* parks. Blacks couldn't swim in *whites only* pools or beaches. Jim Crow laws said that blacks and whites couldn't eat in the same dining rooms in restaurants. Blacks and whites couldn't sleep in the same hotels. Black families couldn't use libraries for white people. There were *whites only* water fountains and *colored only* water fountains. The first time Rosa heard of these fountains she thought "colored" water came in different colors! Rosa learned that the water in both fountains was exactly the same. Rosa wrote, "The difference was who got to drink from which public fountains."

One group of white men, called the Ku Klux Klan, continually threatened African Americans near Rosa's home. The Ku Klux Klan was powerful across America, but especially in the southern states. This was because most African Americans lived in these southern states.

Ku Klux Klan members believed white people were better than black people. They strongly believed black people and white people should be kept apart. The Ku Klux Klan was very active in Pine Level when Rosa was young. These men wore white robes and hoods so no one knew who they were. They rode through black communities scaring people. Often they beat African Americans.

Rosa remembered those frightening days all her life. She said, "The Ku Klux Klan was riding through the black community burning churches, beating up people, killing people."

The students in Rosa's school took everything home each night after school. They never knew if the Ku Klux Klan would burn down their school during the night.

Rosa's grandfather Sylvester often stayed awake at night to protect his family. He sat in his rocking chair by the fireplace. He faced the front door. His gun was nearby. When she felt scared, Rosa sat at her grandfather's feet while he guarded his family. Sometimes Rosa slept in her clothes in case the Ku Klux Klan attacked during the night. This way Rosa would be able to escape quickly. Fortunately, the Ku Klux Klan never attacked Rosa's family. But Rosa spent many sleepless nights in fear of them coming.

Rosa didn't grow up hating white people, however. She said, "I did not grow up feeling that all white people were hateful." Rosa remembers going fishing with an elderly white woman. This lady used to visit Rosa's grandparents and spend time talking with them. Rosa said, "She was real nice and treated us like anybody else."

6
Rosa Works

Rosa had chores to do at home after school. She worked alongside her grandparents and her mother. There were chickens to feed and cows to milk. There was the garden to plant, weed, and harvest. Rosa had fruit to pick. She gathered pecans and walnuts. Since Rosa's family didn't have much money, they grew or made most of what they needed. Rosa's grandfather took extra food to a store in Pine Level to sell or trade. Sometimes Rosa and Sylvester rode in his wagon with him. Grandfather Sylvester sold calves and chickens. He traded eggs for things the family needed, especially cloth for making clothes. Rosa's mother and grandmother made their family's clothes. She watched her mother and grandmother. When Rosa old enough, she cut cloth and sewed cloth Eventually, Rosa became an expert seam-stress.

Rosa earned a little money for her family by picking peanuts, corn, and sweet potatoes on a neighbor's farm. When she was six years old, Rosa began picking cotton, too. When the cotton was tall and the cotton bolls were fluffy white balls, it was time to pick cotton. Rosa carried a flour sack as she went down the cotton rows. Rosa picked bolls of cotton and put them in her sack. Her grandfather expected Rosa to pick two pounds of cotton each day. Each boll didn't weigh very much so it took a lot of cotton to make two pounds.

Rosa and the other black children picking cotton made a game of their work. They raced to see who could pick the most cotton. Rosa added her cotton to what her family col-lected. The cotton was weighed, and the fam-ily was paid by the amount they had picked. Rosa was proud that she could help.

Working in the cotton fields was hot,

backbreaking work. The sun burned Rosa's back. The sand burned her feet.

Rosa worked from sunrise to sunset in the cotton fields. She worked "from can to can't." That means working from when you can see at sunrise until you can't see at sunset. But Rosa's days weren't all filled with work. She relaxed and listened to her grandparents' stories. On Sundays, she went to church. Rosa wrote, "The church, with its musical rhythms and echoes of Africa, thrilled me when I was young."

During her free time, Rosa wandered in the fields and forests around Pine Level. She played in the streams and ponds. She watched deer nibble grass or run off into the forest. Rosa's favorite game was hide-and-seek, which she played with Sylvester and her neighborhood friends. Rosa especially loved to run through fields of blooming wildflowers in May.

One day, when Rosa was eight years old, she went on a trip outside Pine Level. Rosa and her mother went to Montgomery, Alabama, about forty-five miles away. They rode with a friend to Montgomery because black riders sometimes had to ride on the top of buses going between towns!

Rosa's mother went to Montgomery each summer. She took classes so she could keep her teaching certificate. Rosa's mother went to college at Alabama State Normal School, an all-black college. Rosa went to school, too. There was a special school in which college students taught so they could get their teaching certificates. Rosa went to this school while her mother went to college. They lived with relatives in Montgomery.

When Rosa returned home to Pine Level, she was disappointed to learn that her own school had closed. But Rosa was excited, too. Now she and Sylvester would go to the same school where their mother taught!

7
Rosa's New School

Each morning, Rosa and Sylvester got up early to walk to school. They walked eight miles to Spring Hill. After school, they walked eight miles home. The sixteen-mile walk was worth each step because Rosa and Sylvester could see their mother every day. Mrs. McCauley still stayed at a friend's house during the school week while she taught. Rosa's mother taught everything: reading, math, handwriting, science, history, and skills to be used at home.

One day, while Rosa and Sylvester were walking to school, a white boy named Franklin teased them. He called Rosa names. He balled up his fist and threatened to hit Rosa. Rosa wasn't going to put up with this mean behavior. She picked up a brick to defend herself. Franklin saw how serious Rosa was. He backed down.

Grandmother Rose was upset when Rosa told her what had happened. She wasn't upset about Franklin, but with Rosa! She told Rosa to be more careful around white people or she might end up getting badly hurt. Rosa didn't hate white people, she only wanted to be treated fairly. One friend said, "Nobody ever bossed Rosa around and got away with it."

When Rosa was eleven years old, she changed schools again. There was no black middle school or high school for her to attend nearby. If Rosa wanted to finish high school, she would have to move to Montgomery. Rosa went to the Montgomery Industrial School for Girls. This school for African-American girls was more commonly called Miss White's school. Miss White, a white woman from Massachusetts, had started the school to help young black girls get a good education. All the students were black and all the teachers were white. Miss White was the principal.

Rosa finally had her tonsils taken out in Montgomery. Rosa was very sick after the operation. It took her a long time to get well. Rosa missed so much school that she was put into fifth grade instead of sixth grade at Miss White's school. Rosa, however, worked so hard that she was promoted to sixth grade after Christmas!

Rosa stayed with relatives while she was at Miss White's. Her mother paid for her to go to school, but it was difficult. So hard-working Rosa began doing chores at school to help pay for her education. Rosa cleaned blackboards. She dusted desks. She swept floors and emptied trash. Rosa did everything she could to earn money so she could stay at Miss White's school.

Rosa liked Miss White's school. Rosa had white teachers for the first time in her life. Rosa knew some white people treated black people equally.

More than 250 African-American girls at-

tended Miss White's school. They studied reading, English, math, history, science, and geography. The girls took breaks by exercising outside because there were no gym classes. Rosa worked hard to improve her cooking and sewing skills. She knew she would need these skills all her life.

One of Rosa's good friends at Miss White's school was a girl named Johnnie Carr. Rosa and Johnnie remained friends for many years and later worked together to improve the lives of African Americans.

Rosa learned two important lessons at Miss White's school. These were the same lessons Rosa learned from her mother and her grandfather. Rosa learned, "I was a person with dignity and self-respect." Rosa also learned, "I should not set my sights lower than anybody else just because I was black."

Rosa remembered to stand up for herself when she was treated unfairly. One day, when Rosa was walking to Miss White's school, she had a bad experience with a white boy and his mother. Rosa was walking down the sidewalk with her cousins. They were minding their own business because they were passing through a white neighborhood. Suddenly, a white boy came rolling down the sidewalk on his roller skates. He tried to bump Rosa off the sidewalk. Rosa wasn't going to be mistreated this way, so she pushed the white boy. The boy's mother yelled at Rosa. She told Rosa she would send her to jail. Rosa remembers the white woman saying that "she would put me so far in jail that I would never get out again." But Rosa stood up for her rights. She told the woman that her son "had pushed me first and that I didn't want to be pushed, seeing that I wasn't bothering him at all."

One day, Rosa would stand up to a white man who was bullying her. That day she would make history.

8

Rosa's Life Changes

Rosa went to school at Miss White's through eighth grade. Unfortunately, the school closed because Miss White was too old and sick to keep it open any longer. Rosa went to Booker T. Washington Junior High for ninth grade. Then she returned to the school at the college where she had been a summer student. There was no black public high school in Montgomery for Rosa to go to.

Rosa had just begun eleventh grade when her beloved grandmother got sick. Rosa had to make a decision. She desperately wanted to finish high school. But Rosa remembered how much her grandmother loved her. Rosa remembered how her grandmother had cared for her when she was so sick as a child. Rosa knew what she had to do. Rosa was sixteen years old when she left school to take care of her grandmother. Rosa was glad she did. But sadly, her grandmother died after Rosa had been home a month.

Rosa returned to Montgomery. Rosa was an excellent seamstress. In order to support herself, Rosa took a job sewing shirts. She carefully stitched blue-denim work shirts. Rosa also went back to school. But then her mother got sick. Rosa quit her job and quit school. She returned to Pine Level to take care of her mother.

Fortunately, Rosa's brother, Sylvester, was old enough to have a job, which brought in much-needed money. When Rosa's mother got better, Rosa worked cleaning the homes of white people. Rosa remembered her grandfather hadn't wanted his daughters to work in white homes cleaning, cooking, and caring for children. This wasn't a job Rosa wanted to do, but she knew she had to earn money to help her family.

The farm was also Rosa's responsibility.

She cared for the chickens and cows. She planted and harvested the vegetable garden. She picked fruit and collected nuts just like when she was a little girl. All the while, however, Rosa dreamed of finishing high school. Rosa enjoyed being with children. Maybe one day Rosa could become a teacher like her mother.

When Rosa was nineteen years old, she met Raymond Parks. His friends called him "Parks." Parks was nearly ten years older than Rosa. Parks thought Rosa was very interesting even though she was so shy and quiet. Rosa also thought Parks was nice. She enjoyed talking to Parks. She liked listening to Parks tell stories about his life. Parks had been the only black child in his neighborhood. But Parks couldn't go to the local school because it was for white children only. Mrs. Parks taught her son how to read at home.

Just like Rosa, Parks had taken care of his grandmother and his mother when they were sick. Just like Rosa, Parks was eager to learn and improve himself. Just like Rosa, Parks

stood up to white people who treated him unfairly. Rosa said, "Parks believed in being a man and expected to be treated as a man."

Rosa and Parks spent hours talking about relations between black people and white people. Parks was the first man, besides her grandfather Sylvester, with whom she could talk like this. He was actively working to help black people. Parks was a member of the National Association for the Advancement of Colored People, commonly called the NAACP. Rosa admired Parks' courage and determination. She wrote, "Parks was always interested and willing to work for things that would improve life for his race, his family, and himself."

Rosa loved Parks. Parks loved Rosa. In December 1932, Rosa and Parks were married. Rosa was nineteen years old. Rosa and Parks were married in Rosa's home in Pine Level. Rosa McCauley was now Rosa Parks, a name that would go down in history.

9
Rosa Works
for Equal Rights

Rosa and Parks moved to Montgomery, Alabama. Parks cut hair in a barbershop. Rosa went back to high school. In 1933, when Rosa was twenty years old, she graduated from high school. Parks was there to see Rosa's dream finally come true. But, even with a high school diploma, Rosa couldn't get a good job because she was black. Rosa worked as a hospital helper. She took in sewing jobs to earn extra money.

In 1941, Rosa got a new job at Maxwell Field, an Army Air Force base. On the base, for the first time in her life, Rosa could sit wherever she wanted to on the buses and trolleys. President Franklin D. Roosevelt had ordered that segregation be ended in public places on military bases. But off the base, life was the same. Rosa wrote, "I could ride on an integrated trolley on the base, but when I left the base, I had to ride home on a segregated bus."

Rosa liked President Roosevelt and his wife, Eleanor. She wanted to vote to reelect President Roosevelt. But first, Rosa had to register to vote. Although African Americans were allowed to vote, many restrictions made it very difficult. They had to register, but only at special times. They had to take a special test. They had to pay a voting tax. Even with these obstacles, Rosa made up her mind to vote.

In 1943, Rosa went to register. She took the test. She waited for her voter's card. It never came. When she asked why, Rosa was told she had failed the test. Rosa worked with NAACP state president Edgar Daniel Nixon to encourage more African Americans to register to vote. In 1945, Rosa took the test again. But this time, she wrote down all of her answers and brought them home with her. Rosa knew she had passed. If she didn't get her voter's card, she would go to court with her answers to prove she had passed the test.

Rosa finally got her voter's card. She was thirty-two years old. But Rosa had to pay a voting tax of $16.50. That was $1.50 for each year she could have voted since she turned twenty-one years old. That was a lot of money for Rosa, but she paid it. When Rosa voted for the first time she "felt a lot of bother to do something so simple and uneventful." But Rosa had followed all the unfair rules and had reached her goal of voting.

One day, however, Rosa didn't follow the rules. She was riding on a Montgomery bus when she stood up to a mean bus driver who picked on black people. His name was James Blake. Rosa knew that the buses had special rules. One rule was that the first ten seats were reserved for white riders. The back ten seats were for black riders. The sixteen seats in the middle could be used by either race.

But if a black person was sitting and a white person was standing, all the black people in that row had to get up to give one seat to one white person. Another rule was that black riders had to pay their fare at the front door, get off the bus, and walk to the back door in order to ride. The bus drivers carried guns to enforce the segregation laws.

One winter day, Rosa waited for a bus after work. When the bus rolled up, Rosa saw that the back was crowded. She wouldn't be able to squeeze in at the back door where blacks were supposed to get on. Rosa went in the front door of the bus and paid her money. But instead of getting off again to go through the back door, Rosa simply walked down the aisle to the black section.

Mr. Blake, the bus driver, got very angry. He told Rosa to get off the bus and go to the back door. Rosa said, "I was already on the bus and didn't see the need of getting off and getting back on." Mr. Blake told her to get off the bus. Rosa said, "I will get off." She dropped her purse and sat down on a front seat to

pick it up. Mr. Blake acted like he was going to hit Rosa. Rosa looked him in the eye and said, "I know one thing. You better not hit me." Rosa took a good look at Mr. Blake. She didn't want to forget his face. Rosa said, "I never wanted to be on that bus again." Then Rosa Parks proudly stepped off the bus.

For the next twelve years, Rosa checked out each bus driver before she boarded his bus. Rosa refused to ride any bus driven by James Blake. During these years, Rosa became more involved in the movement for equal rights. She worked part-time as a seamstress for a white couple, Virginia and Clifford Durr. They encouraged her to learn more about taking a stand. Rosa even attended a workshop for community leaders at the Highlander School in the summer of 1955.

One day later in 1955 Rosa Parks took a bus and forgot to look to see who the driver was. She accidentally climbed on James Blake's bus and made history.

10
Rosa Makes Her Stand

The day Rosa Parks made her stand by sitting was Thursday, December 1, 1955. Rosa was forty-two years old. Rosa rode the Cleveland Avenue bus to her job as a seamstress in downtown Montgomery. She was very busy that December. She had joined the NAACP and was secretary. She ran a youth group helping young African Americans. She taught Sunday school and helped at her church. Five days a week, she sewed women's dresses, stitched men's suits, and ironed and pressed clothes in a department store.

On December 1, Rosa was planning a special NAACP meeting in town for that weekend. She was thinking about the Christmas season. A little after five o'clock, Rosa's workday was over. She was tired and her body ached. Rosa didn't get on the first bus that came by. It was too crowded. Rosa went to a drugstore to buy some Christmas presents, toothpaste, and aspirin. On her way back to the bus stop, Rosa wondered if Parks had had a good day at work. She wondered what her mother had cooked for dinner. She thought about the NAACP meeting she would go to that evening. Rosa was so busy thinking that, when the next bus stopped, she forgot to check who was driving it. Rosa paid her dime, got on the bus, and walked to the black section at the back of the bus.

Only then did Rosa realize that the bus driver was none other than James Blake! He was the driver who had made Rosa get off the bus twelve years earlier. He was the one she never wanted to ride with again. Rosa sat down in the first open seat in the black part of the bus. But as more white riders got on, the seats in the white section filled up. One white man was left standing. James Blake told Rosa and the other three black riders in her row, "Y'all better make it light on your-selves and let me have those seats."

The three other black riders got up. Rosa moved over to a window seat. Rosa Parks had made up her mind not to give up her seat. She remembered how her grandfather had stood up for his rights. Rosa was ready to stand up for her rights by sitting down. The bus driver asked Rosa if she was going to stand up. Rosa said, "No." The driver said, "Well, I'm going to have you arrested." Rosa replied, "You may do that." The driver called the police to arrest Rosa Parks.

Later, Rosa was asked why she didn't stand up. Rosa answered, "I was not tired physically, or no more tired than I usually was at the end of a working day. No, the only tired I was, was tired of giving in." When two police officers came, Rosa asked, "Why do you all push us around?" One officer answered, "I don't know, but the law is the law and you are under arrest." Rosa was taken to the police station, fingerprinted, and put into a cell. Rosa was thirsty but couldn't have

a drink of water from the *whites only* water fountain. After a long time, Rosa was allowed to call Parks. Parks and several friends came to get Rosa out of jail.

Rosa was going to have to go to court on Monday, December 5. Word spread quickly throughout the black community about Rosa's arrest. Black leaders decided to highlight Rosa's arrest by boycotting the buses all day Monday. That meant that no black riders were supposed to ride the buses to work, shop, or school that day. Rosa knew she wouldn't be riding. She promised herself never to ride another segregated bus!

Rosa was asked if her arrest could be used as a test case against segregation. Rosa discussed it with Parks and her mother. They knew it would be dangerous, but they agreed. Rosa should take her stand and fight segregation even if it meant taking her case all the way to the U.S. Supreme Court. A special committee was created to help organize the bus boycott. Twenty-six-year-old Dr. Martin

Luther King, Jr., was selected to run the committee.

No one knew if the black community would really rally behind Rosa or not. But the answer came on Monday when bus after bus rolled through Montgomery with no black riders. The boycott was a success! Rosa went to court and was fined fourteen dollars. Someone in the crowd that had gathered to support Rosa said, "They've messed with the wrong one now." Soon the crowd was chanting, "They've messed with the wrong one now." The crowd was right!

That night Dr. King and other black leaders called a meeting to see if the boycott should be continued. Black people filled the church where the meeting was held. Thousands more stood outside. Dr. King gave a short speech about Rosa's brave stand against segregation. Dr. King said, "I'm happy it happened to a person like Rosa Parks, for nobody can doubt the boundless reach of her integrity." When Dr. King asked for people to stand who agreed that the bus boycott should continue, everyone in the audience stood. Dr. King gave Rosa a big hug.

That night, neither Rosa Parks nor Dr. King realized that they had begun a civil rights movement that would end segregation. The bus boycott was a long, difficult struggle. But the black community held together and stayed off the buses. Finally, 381 days after the boycott began, the Supreme Court ruled that segregation on Montgomery's buses was against the law.

Shy, quiet Rosa Parks had taken her stand against segregation by keeping her seat and had won! But many white people were upset with Rosa. They made threats against her. Things got so bad that Rosa, Parks, and her mother moved to Detroit, where her brother, Sylvester, lived, to escape the threats.

For the rest of her life, Rosa worked to make things better for black people. She helped many young people, too. After Parks died, Rosa set up the Rosa and Raymond Parks Institute for Self-Development. Rosa wanted her young black friends to have a chance to improve their education and their lives. Rosa said, "I would like them to have the same sense of home, dignity, and pride that was instilled in me by my family and my teachers."

This was one of Rosa's proudest achievements. Rosa was also proud to have been given many honorary college degrees for her civil rights work. Leaders around the world praised Rosa for her brave stand and followed her example. And today Cleveland Avenue, the street on which Rosa traveled by bus, has been renamed Rosa Parks Boulevard.

Rosa Parks had this dream. She wished for "everyone living together in peace and harmony and love . . . that's the goal we seek, and I think that the more people there are who reach that state of mind, the better we will all be." On that warm February morning in 1913, who would have guessed that tiny Rosa McCauley would one day make such a gigantic change in America's history?